Mystical Cats in Secret Places

A CAT LOVER'S COLORING BOOK

Illustrations by
Honoel

Waves of Color

Mystical Cats in Secret Places: A Cat Lover's Coloring Book
© 2016 Seven Seas Entertainment, LLC.
All rights reserved.

Artwork: Honoel A. Ibardolaza
Art Assistants: Mariz Eloisa Hechanova & Christian Pamotillo
Cover Coloring: Ma. Victoria Robado
Logo Design: Courtney Williams
Cover Design: Nicky Lim
Production Manager: Lissa Pattillo
Editor-in-Chief: Adam Arnold
Publisher: Jason DeAngelis

Waves of Color books may be purchased in bulk for educational, business, or promotional use. For information on bulk purchases, please contact Macmillan Corporate & Premium Sales Department at 1-800-221-7945 (ext 5442) or write specialmarkets@macmillan.com.

ISBN: 978-1-626923-95-9

Printed in Canada

First Printing: June 2016

10 9 8 7 6 5 4 3 2 1

WISHING WELL

Illustration Index

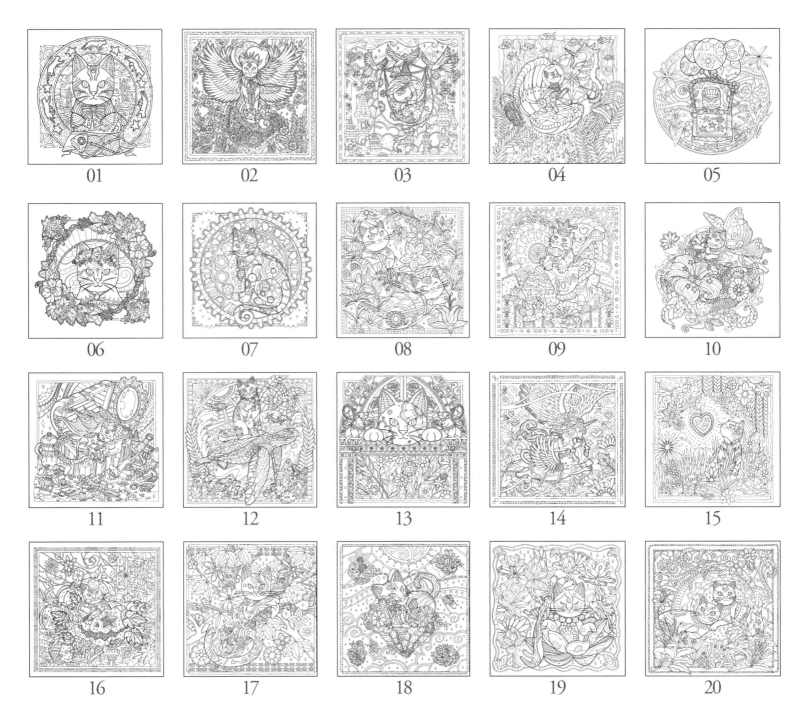

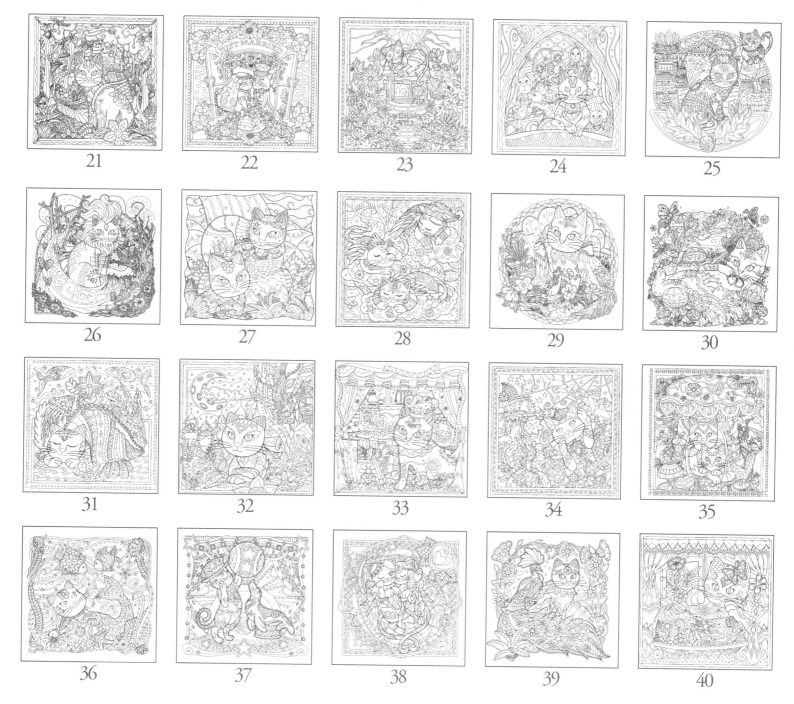

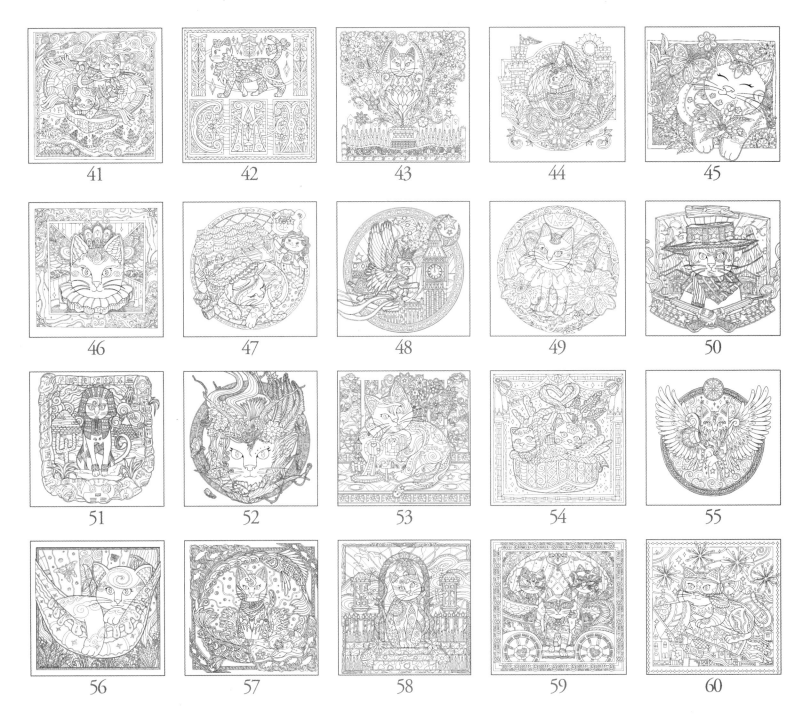

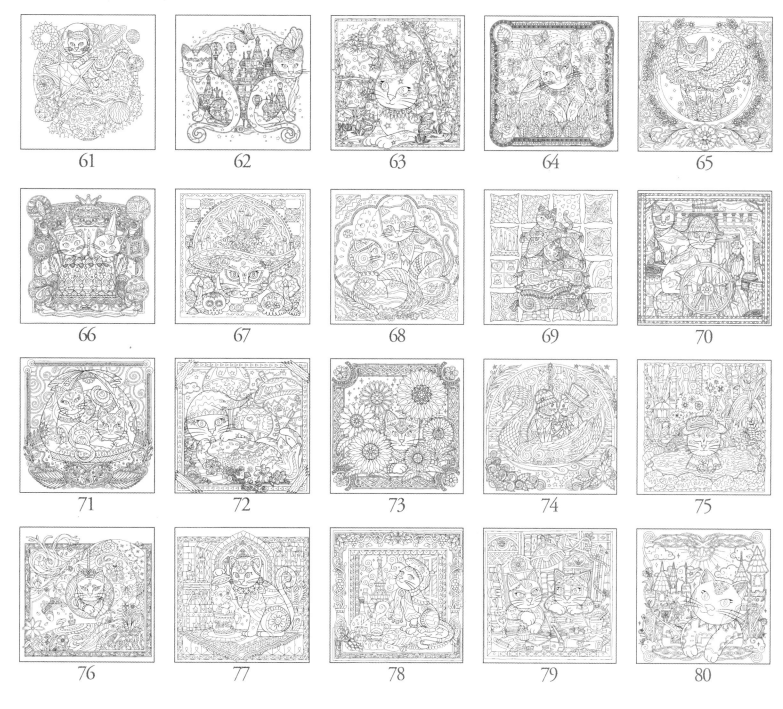

61   62   63   64   65

66   67   68   69   70

71   72   73   74   75

76   77   78   79   80